Reporting from the front line

A special band of brothers braved the First World War without weapons, instead armed with cameras and a determination to expose the bloody reality of the conflict.

These photographers chronicled the horrors in groundbreaking images.

Among them were three brothers from London's East End employed by the Daily Mirror. On the day war broke out in August 1914, Tom, Horace and Bernard Grant were on holiday on the south coast and headed straight to Belgium.

Youngest brother Bernard summed up the life of a war photographer in memoirs To The Four Corners. He wrote: "I have never ceased to wonder at the things that I, and other Fleet Street men, were able to do in those early days of the war. We used to motor out in search of photographs, often passing into No Man's Lands. Why we were never captured will for ever be a mystery."

Mirror man Ernest Brooks was the first and longest-serving British war photographer and took 4,400 images on the Western Front, in Italy and at Gallipoli.

And Ivor Castle took some 800 photographs between 1916 and 1917, including pictures of the first tank, which the Mirror published in November 1916.

In World War Two, when the editor called across the Mirror newsroom for a volunteer to join British troops, a young reporter eagerly raised his hand.

Scots-born Ian Fyfe, 25, wanted to be the first British journalist into France as Europe was liberated from Nazi occupation. Military contacts won him a seat in a glider set to land men from 9th Parachute Battalion under cover of darkness.

But Ian's glider was shot down, no wreckage ever recovered and like so many fallen soldiers, neither was Ian's body.

Ian is named in the Reporters Without Borders garden in Bayeux, France, which also has an inscription for the Sunday Mirror's Rupert Hamer, who died in Afghanistan in 2010. War reporter Bernard Gray of the Sunday Pictorial, which in 1963 became the Sunday Mirror, was the only Second World War journalist to die in a British submarine. He was on HMS Urge sailing from Malta to Egypt in May 1942 when it was bombed by enemy planes.

All these brave journalists, photographers and writers risked – and in the most tragic cases – gave their lives to bring reality to readers about conflicts where truth is often the first casualty.

CONTENTS

7 INTRODUCTION
Our treasure trove of images, hand curated to commemorate 80 years since VE Day.

15 WAR BREAKS OUT
Adolf Hitler invades Poland, igniting a conflagration which engulfed the world.

42 PEARL HARBOR
A surprise attack which shocked the United States and brought it into World War Two.

48 THE EASTERN FRONT
Germany versus the USSR was the bloodiest and most brutal theatre of war.

68 THE HOLOCAUST
We must never forget six million Jews and millions of others were murdered by Nazi Germany.

78 VICTORY
After more than five hard years of war, the evil spectre of fascism was defeated.

88 NAGASAKI AND HIROSHIMA
The first - and only - use of atomic weapons during a time of war.

PICTURES FROM:
Mirrorpix
Joe Rosenthal/AP,
Robert Capa/
Magnum Photos,
Getty Images,
TT News
Agency/AKG,
Bridgeman Images,
Shutterstock,
The Imperial War
Museum

Photographs curated by: John Mead & Ivor Game
Designer: Julia Mans
Commissioning Editor: Clare Fitzsimons
Operations Manager: Nick Moreton
Marketing and Communications Manager: Claire Brown
Printed by: Micropress
ISBN: 9781917439527

INTRODUCTION

Portraits of a world at war

May 8 2025 is a chance to look back 80 years, hearts full of gratitude to those who made the ultimate sacrifice so we could live in a free world.

It is also one of the last times we will do so alongside the lucky ones who made it home from World War Two.

We will remember them all in this 80th anniversary of VE Day special commemorative tribute.

The Reach picture archive contains 200 million images. Carefully chosen from this treasure trove are these 50 handpicked historical photographs – including many rarely seen shots – which capture the devastating moments, horror, hope and eventual triumph of the conflict which raged from 1939 to 1945.

The rise of Adolf Hitler's Reich, to the outbreak of war and invasions across the continent. Images of conflict from Dunkirk to the Battle of Britain are interspersed with the reality of life for so many - young children being evacuated, those huddled inside London's underground during the Blitz, Land Girls trying to keep the nation fed and a couple simply sharing a kiss.

The unimaginable horror of Auschwitz and the blood-soaked beaches of Normandy lead, via a devastating path, to the unbridled joy of VE Day and eventually, to VJ Day and the end of the conflict.

With loving care Head of Archives John Mead and Picture Editor Ivor Game scoured 25,000 images of World War Two.

Choosing only 50 to tell the story of a conflict that changed the world forever was a huge but important task.

Ivor says: "John and myself have tried to tell the story of World War Two from the point of view of the people.

"From the wealth of pictures within the Daily Mirror, Daily Express, and the Reach national and regional picture archives, we can get a glimpse of their lives, try to tell their stories, through the war photographers and reporters who witnessed first hand how quickly a conflict can become global.

"In the 50 pictures in this book, we hope to show that people need each other and that ultimately war can never be the answer."

1936 After Adolf Hitler became Chancellor of Germany in 1933, the Nazi party staged rallies in Nuremberg over the next five years, parading the country's military might for propaganda purposes. Here, in September 1936, patriotism reached fever pitch after Hitler had defied the treaties following World One and remilitarised the Rhineland bordering France only a few months earlier.

1938 Keen to avoid war with an increasingly belligerent Germany, Britain and France persuaded Czechoslovakia to hand over the Sudetenland – home to a large ethnic German population – to Hitler without a bullet being fired. In early October 1938 the Führer, accompanied by tanks, planes and thousands of troops, arrived in triumph in the region.

1938 *Having persuaded Czechoslovakia to hand over Sudetenland to pacify Hitler, British Prime Minister Neville Chamberlain arrived home waving the piece of paper signed at the Munich Agreement and declaring it meant "peace for our time". Sadly this policy of appeasement failed and in 1940 Chamberlain was replaced as PM by Winston Churchill.*

1939 *His fellow Brits look unconcerned, as a cigarette smoking Sunday Dispatch newspaper vendor holds a bill announcing Britain is now at war with Germany, on September 3 1939.*

War breaks out

World War Two began when Nazi Germany invaded Poland. Adolf Hitler had already taken over Austria and Czechoslovakia, but the invasion of Poland crossed a line for Britain and France, who had promised to defend it if attacked. Both nations declared war on Germany on September 3, 1939.

But the seeds of the immense conflict were sown two decades earlier.

Germany felt bitter and humiliated after its World War One defeat and treatment by the victors. The 1919 Treaty of Versailles was extremely harsh on the loser, forcing Germany to accept full responsibility, pay huge reparations, lose territory, and disarm.

The punishing combination – along with a global depression – led to such hyperinflation people used wheelbarrows to carry money, as well as massive unemployment and widespread poverty.

This was the perfect environment for populist extremist Hitler to gain support. He promised to undo the Treaty of Versailles, and, in modern parlance, make Germany great again.

In Britain, the declaration of war was announced by Prime Minister Neville Chamberlain on the Home Service: "I am speaking to you from the Cabinet Room at 10, Downing Street.

"This morning the British Ambassador in Berlin handed the German Government a final Note stating that unless we heard from them by 11 o'clock that they were prepared at once to withdraw their troops from Poland a state of war would exist between us.

"I have to tell you now that no such undertaking has been received, and that consequently this country is at war with Germany."

1940 In one of the most famous images of the war, Nazi soldiers herd terrified Jewish men, women and children full of "tremendous dread", out of the Warsaw Ghetto to an extermination camp. At one point, almost half a million Jews were imprisoned, starving, in this small area of the Polish capital before being sent to death camps. 300,000 were either gassed or shot during 1943's Warsaw Ghetto Uprising, with another 92,000 dying of starvation or disease. The SS soldier with the machine gun was identified as Josef Blösche, executed in 1969 for atrocities thanks to this picture.

1940 *In just three days as war broke out in 1939, 1.5 million children were evacuated from our major cities to the countryside to escape feared German bombing. Another wave of evacuations occurred a year later as the Blitz began, including these Birmingham evacuees who arrived at Ripley station on November 15 1940.*

1940 After much dithering, in April 1940 Britain and France agreed to mine shipping routes in Norway to stop Swedish iron ore reaching Germany. By then, Germany had decided to invade Norway and Denmark and did so with clinical efficiency. Denmark was conquered in a day. Norway – including these troops advancing along a valley road – took until June.

1940 Almost all of Europe was aflame as Germany invaded France and the Low Countries on May 10 1940 - the same day Winston Churchill became Prime Minister. Here Nazi troops are seen in a small blazing village in north eastern France, in June 1940. France fell in the third week of that month, beaten by a smaller but more modern German army.

1940 With the French army on the run, the British Expeditionary Force had to fall back to Dunkirk. Protected by the RAF and Royal Navy, an incredible 338,000 Allied troops were rescued during the Dunkirk Evacuation between May 26 and June 4 1940, many in Little Ships from across the Channel. Sadly, 90,000 were also taken prisoner, and most tanks and heavy guns were lost.

1940 *Essentially it was a defeat, but the rescue of so many troops from the jaws of defeat was hailed as a "miracle" by Churchill and the nation celebrated the return of Our Boys as a victory. Here, relieved troops on a train enjoy a drink to toast their escape from the Nazis.*

1940 *German troops parade down the Champs-Elysees after the fall of Paris in June 14 1940. The French decided not to fight in the capital to spare "it the devastation which defence would have involved". Eight days later France surrendered.*

1940 *The Battle of Britain between "the few" of the RAF and the Luftwaffe began on July 10 1940. Pictured on July 29, relaxing on the grass beside their Hawker Hurricane Mk1 fighters on the airfield at RAF Hawkinge near Folkestone, Kent, are (L-R) Flying Officer Rupert Smythe (wounded in action 24.08.40), Pilot Officer Keith Gillman (killed in action 25.08.40), Pilot Officer John Proctor, Flying Officer Peter Brothers, Pilot Officer Douglas Grice (wounded in action 15.08.40), Flying Officer Peter Gardner (taken prisoner 11.07.41) and Flying Officer Alan Eckford of 'B' Flight, No. 32 Squadron RAF Fighter Command.*

1941

A popular slogan during World War Two was: "Carrots help you see in the blackout." The night-time success of the RAF was also credited to carrots to keep the invention of radar secret. The use of radio waves to detect objects beyond sight range had been developed by British scientists and engineers during the 1930s. It was known as radar - 'radio detection and ranging'. By 1939, a chain of early warning radar stations were built along the south and east coasts of Britain. Radar could pick up enemy aircraft 80 miles away and played a crucial role in the Battle of Britain. The radar stations sent their information into The Filter Room at RAF Bentley Priory Headquarters Fighter Command which then forwarded it onto The Operations Room, the only place which oversaw all aerial movements above Britain. Here, in The Operations Room, members of the Women's Auxiliary Air Force plot aircraft movements in June 1941, ensuring scrambled RAF pilots can intercept enemy raids.

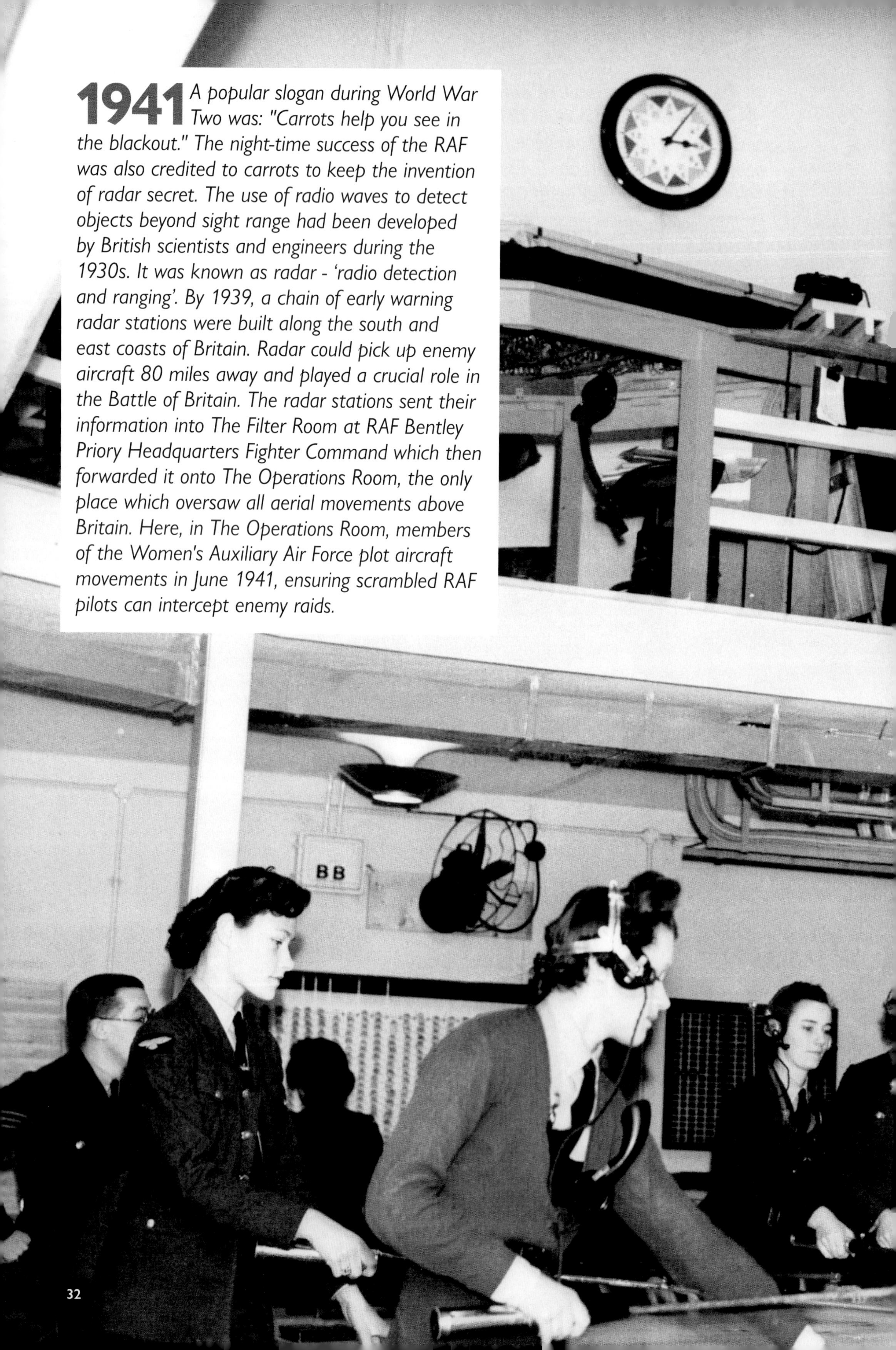

1941 On the first day of the Blitz on September 7 1940, a Heinkel He 111 bomber flies over the Isle of Dogs in the East End of London, now the location of Canary Wharf, home of the Daily Mirror and Daily Express newspapers.

1941 Londoners use Aldwych Underground Station as an air raid shelter during bomb attacks on London during the Second World War. An estimated 177,000 people bedded down in the Tube during the Blitz air raids.

TO STAGE AND EXIT

NO VISITORS ALLOWED IN DRESSING ROOMS AT ANY TIME

1940

A Windmill Girl kisses her RAF pilot boyfriend backstage at the Windmill Theatre, London, home to a very risque but patriotic revue, in September 1940.

1944 *At its peak in 1944, more than 80,000 women — often known as 'land girls' — were in the Women's Land Army, helping to boost the country's food production. Rats eat grain, so this land girl, pictured in March 1944, worked as a rat catcher and looking at that haul a very good one too.*

1941 *The American destroyer USS Shaw explodes during the Japanese attack on Pearl Harbor, home of the American Pacific Fleet on December 7 1941. The attack led to the United States entering World War Two.*

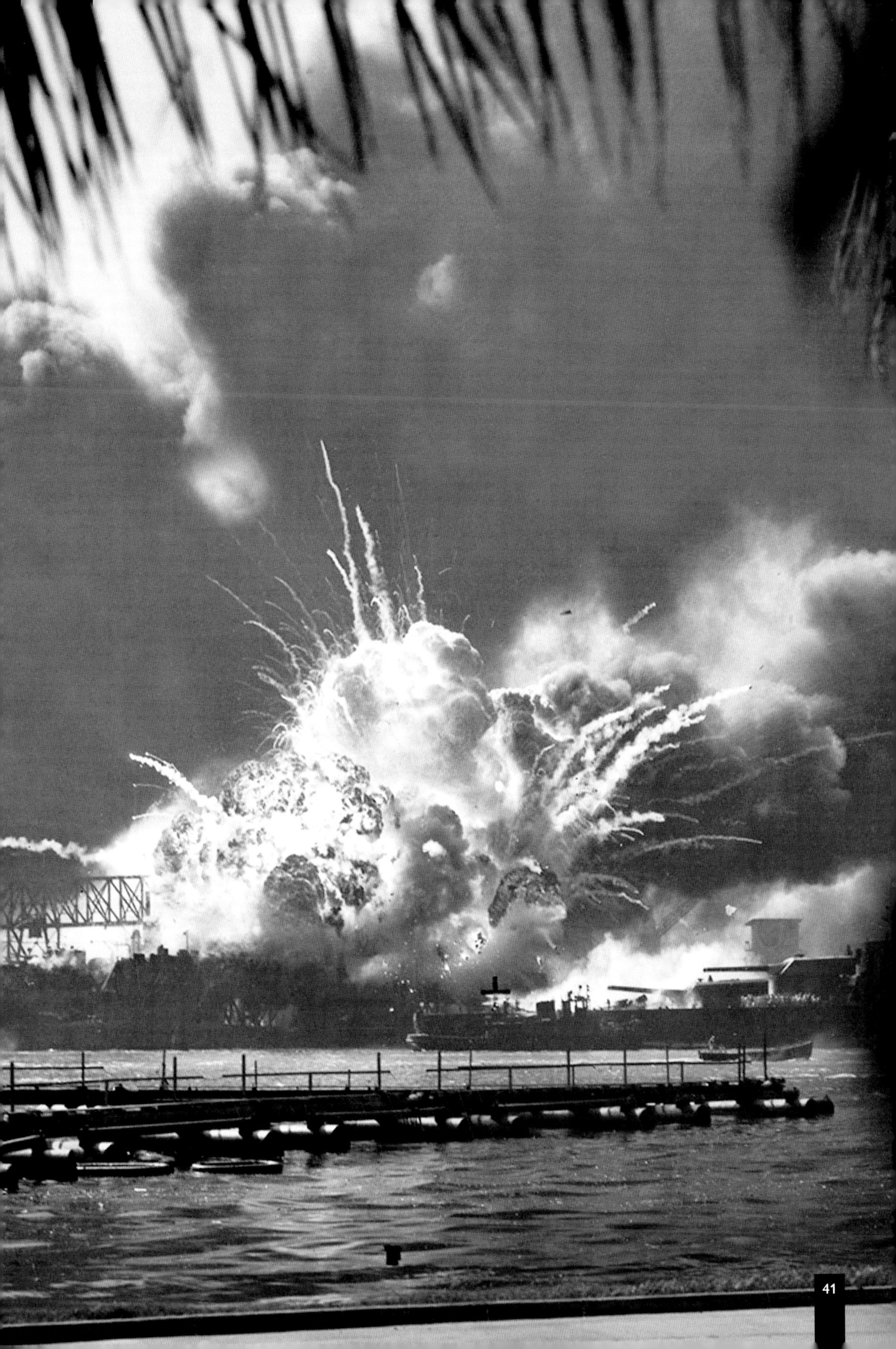

Pearl Harbor

The US President Franklin D Roosevelt called December 7 1941, "a date which will live in infamy". At 7.55am Hawaiian time two waves of Japanese fighters and bombers launched a surprise attack on the United States of America's naval base at Pearl Harbor.

World war had raged in other parts of the globe for more than two years but until then, officially at least, the US was at peace. That changed after 2,343 service personnel were killed, 151 planes destroyed on the ground and all eight US battleships at anchor sunk or damaged.

Japan intended the first blow to be crippling and lead to a short war and decisive victory but American industrial might prevented that. But it did seriously affect the morale of the population across the 50 states. So, in April 1942 the US launched the daring Doolittle Raid to bomb Tokyo.

1942 A US Navy Douglas SBD Dauntless scout and dive bomber drops a message container known as a "bean-bag" on the flight deck of the USS Enterprise while crew members dart to catch the message to deliver it up to the ship's bridge during the Doolittle Raid to bomb Tokyo in April 1942.

1942 *A US destroyer fires a pattern of depth charges during a search for a German U-boat on November 9 1942. The depth charge was the main anti-submarine weapon used against the German submarines during the Battle of the Atlantic. Invented in 1911, they destroy or cripple a sub with a powerful hydraulic shock caused by an underwater detonation.*

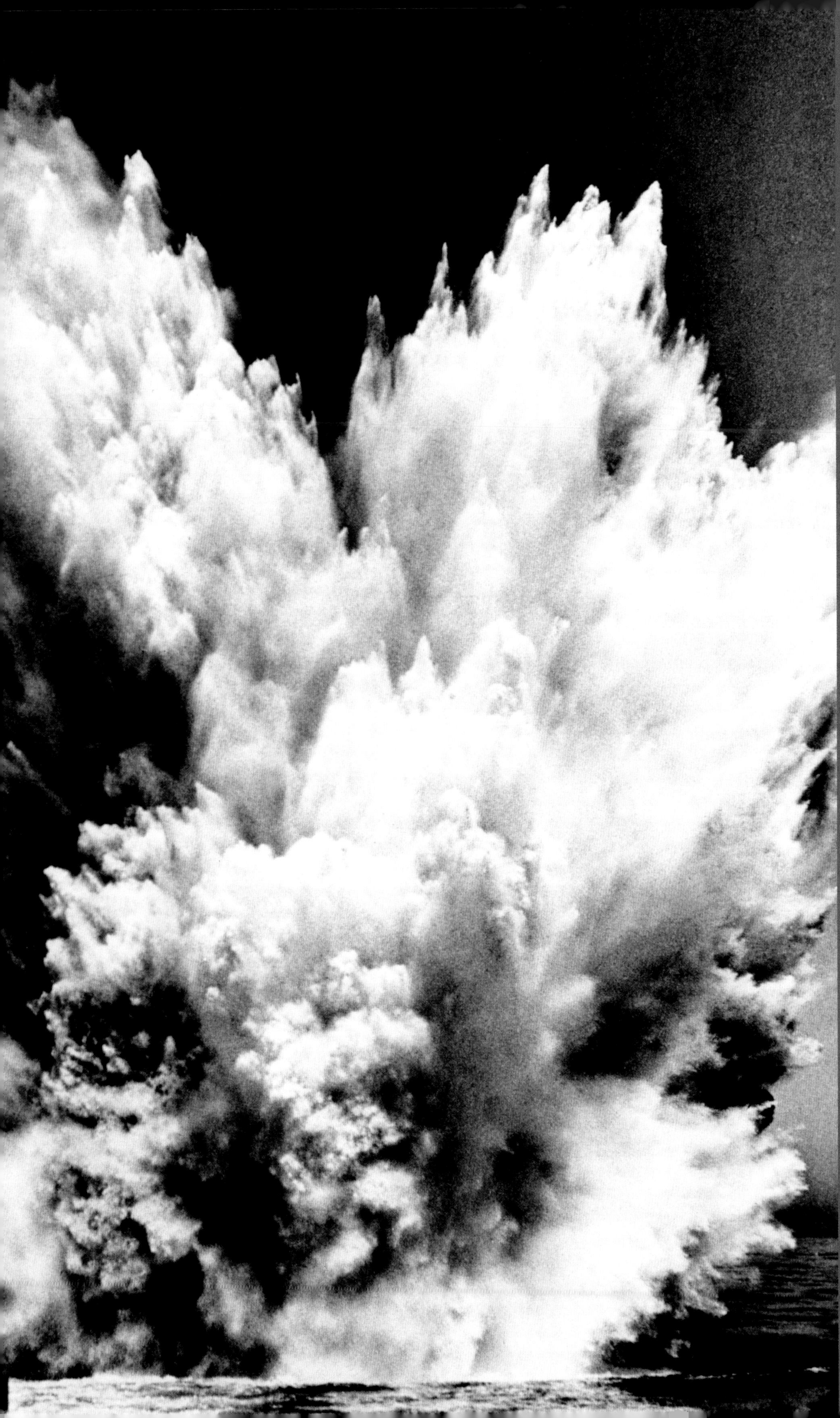

1943 Hitler launched Operation Barbarossa, the German invasion of the Soviet Union, on June 22, 1941. The Siege of Leningrad – now St Petersburg – lasted for 872 days, without the city falling. It was the most destructive in history and caused an estimated 1.5 million deaths. Here women take water from a broken water main.

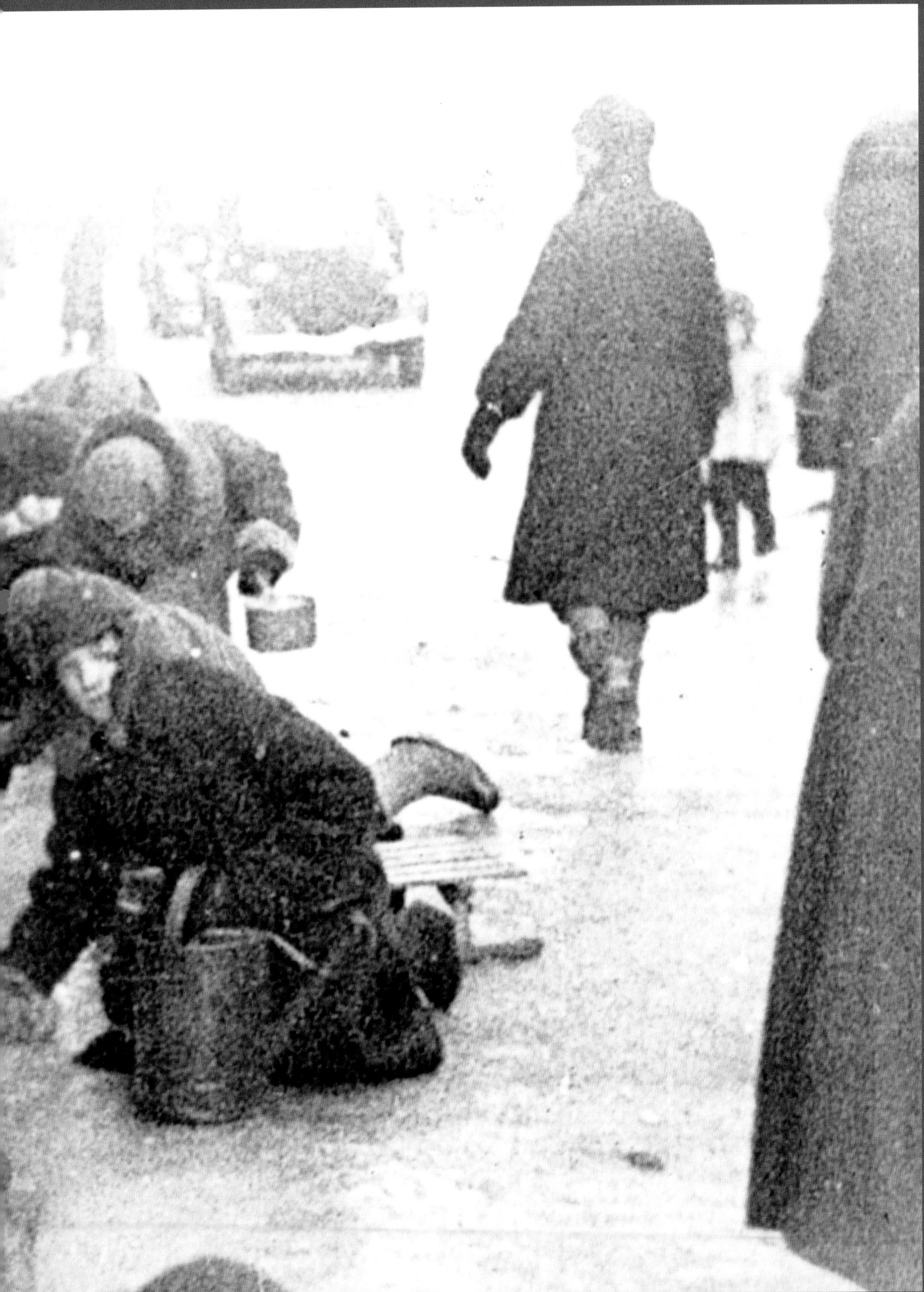

The Eastern Front

This was World War Two's largest and bloodiest theatre of combat, stretching from the Baltic to the Black Sea. It began on June 22 1941 with Operation Barbarossa, when Nazi Germany launched a massive invasion of the Soviet Union. The Axis forces numbered over three million and the initial German advance was rapid, but the harsh Russian winter and fierce Soviet resistance halted their progress near Moscow.

The tide turned in 1942 with the Battle of Stalingrad, where the Red Army encircled and defeated the German 6th Army.

In 1943, the Battle of Kursk became the largest tank battle in history. The Germans launched Operation Citadel, but the Soviets, anticipating the attack, launched counteroffensives that led to a decisive victory.

The war on the Eastern Front was horrifically brutal, with both sides suffering immense casualties. Estimates of Soviet military deaths reach as high as 10 million, and civilian casualties between 18 and 24 million.

1943 *The first major setback for Germany came with the surrender of the German Sixth Army after the Battle of Stalingrad. Here Germans wave the white flag to USSR Red Army soldiers in January 1943. During the battle almost 150,000 Germans were killed and wounded, and more than 91,000 captured. Only 5,000 survived Soviet PoW camps. It's estimated there were 1.1million Soviet casualties.*

1941 *The Western Desert Campaign took place in Egypt and Libya, the main theatre in the North African campaign, which saw the Allies including the British 7th Armoured Division known as the Desert Rats under the likes of Bernard Montgomery face off against Erwin Rommel's Afrika Korps. Here, men of the Imperial Australian Forces are on manoeuvres in the Libyan desert in January 1941.*

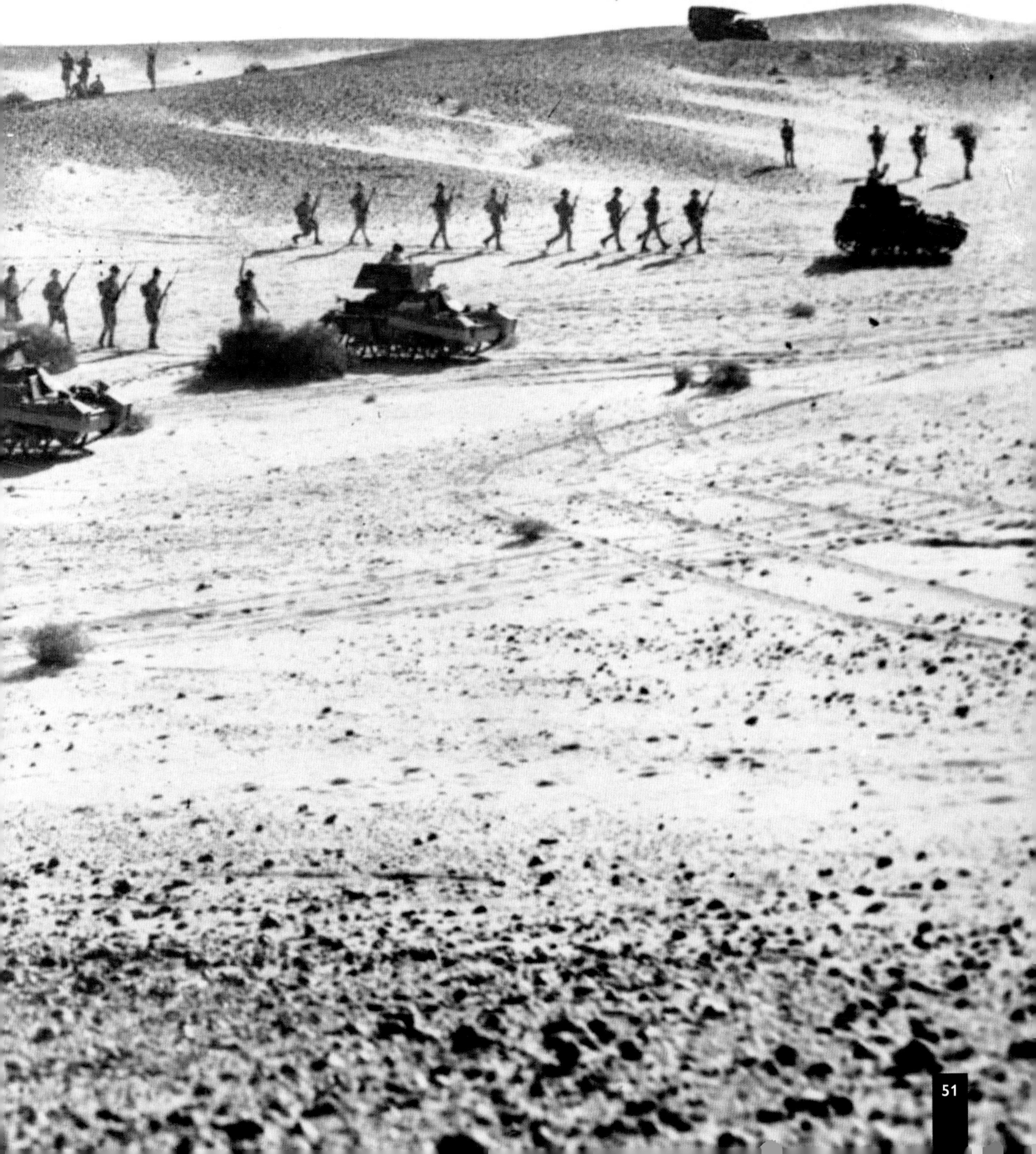

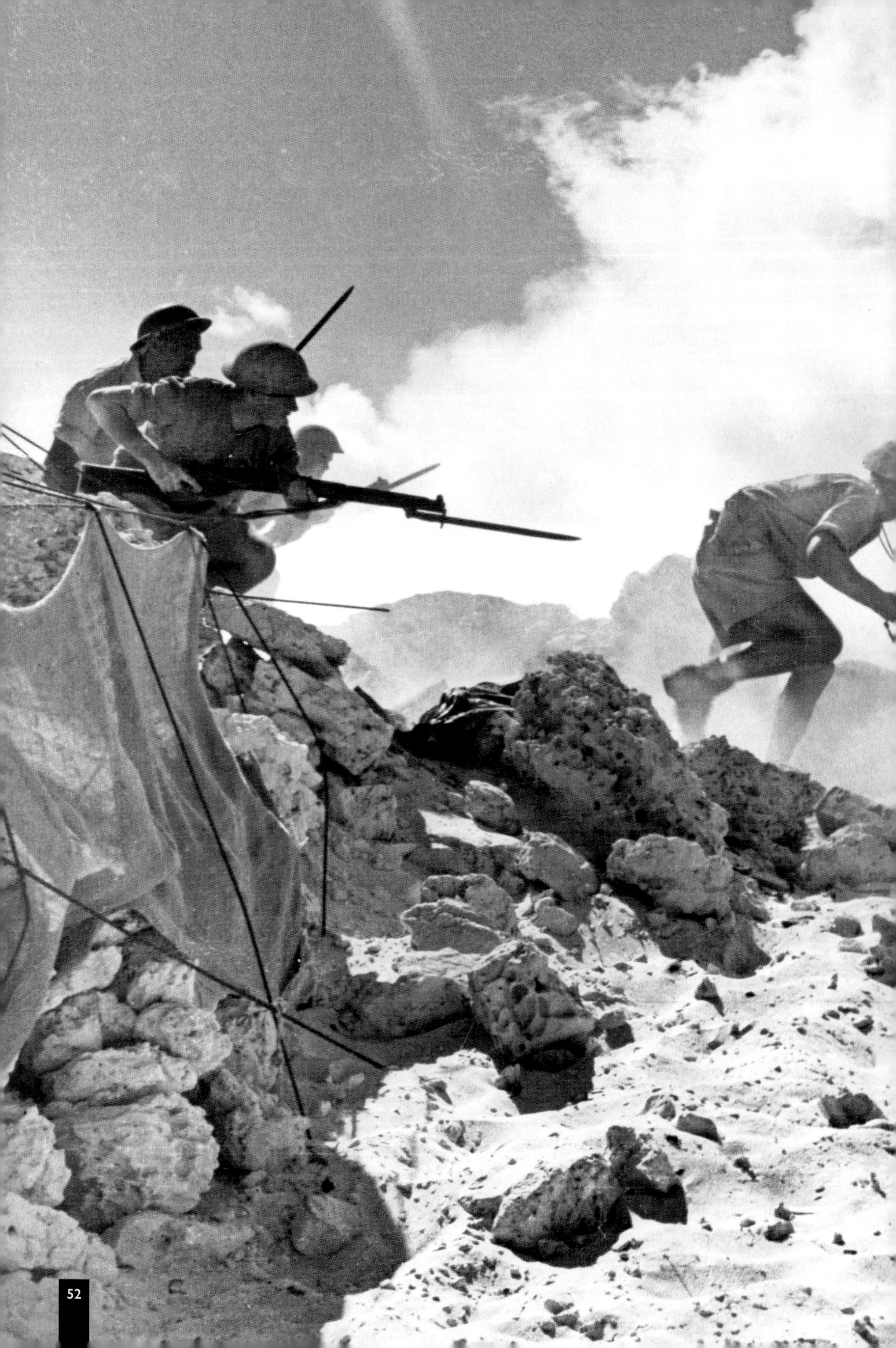

1942 British infantry attack enemy positions under cover of a smokescreen at the Second Battle of El Alamein in November 1942. The Allied victory ended the Axis threat to the Middle East.

1943 RAF and USAAF bombers practically obliterated Hamburg during July and August 1943. Codenamed Operation Gomorrah, it created a huge firestorm, killing 37,000 people, wounding 180,000, and destroying 60% of the city's houses.

55

56

1943 An RAF Avro Lancaster of Bomber Command is silhouetted against flares, smoke and explosions during a 148 aircraft attack on Hamburg, Germany, on the night of January 30 1943. Fifty-eight people were killed and five aircraft were lost.

1944 The Allied invasion of mainland Italy began on September 3 1943. At the beginning of 1944, the Allies were heading for Rome but first came the Battle of Monte Cassino, a series of four assaults by Allied Forces against the Axis-held mountainous Winter Line. Here soldiers of the New Zealand army are pictured amongst the ruins of the town of Cassino during the battle in February 1944.

1943 *A Soviet T34 tank bearing the words "For the Motherland" accompanies Red Army troops on the Eastern Front. 80,000 T34s were built, making it the most produced tank of the war. With 44,900 lost or damaged, it also suffered the most tank losses ever.*

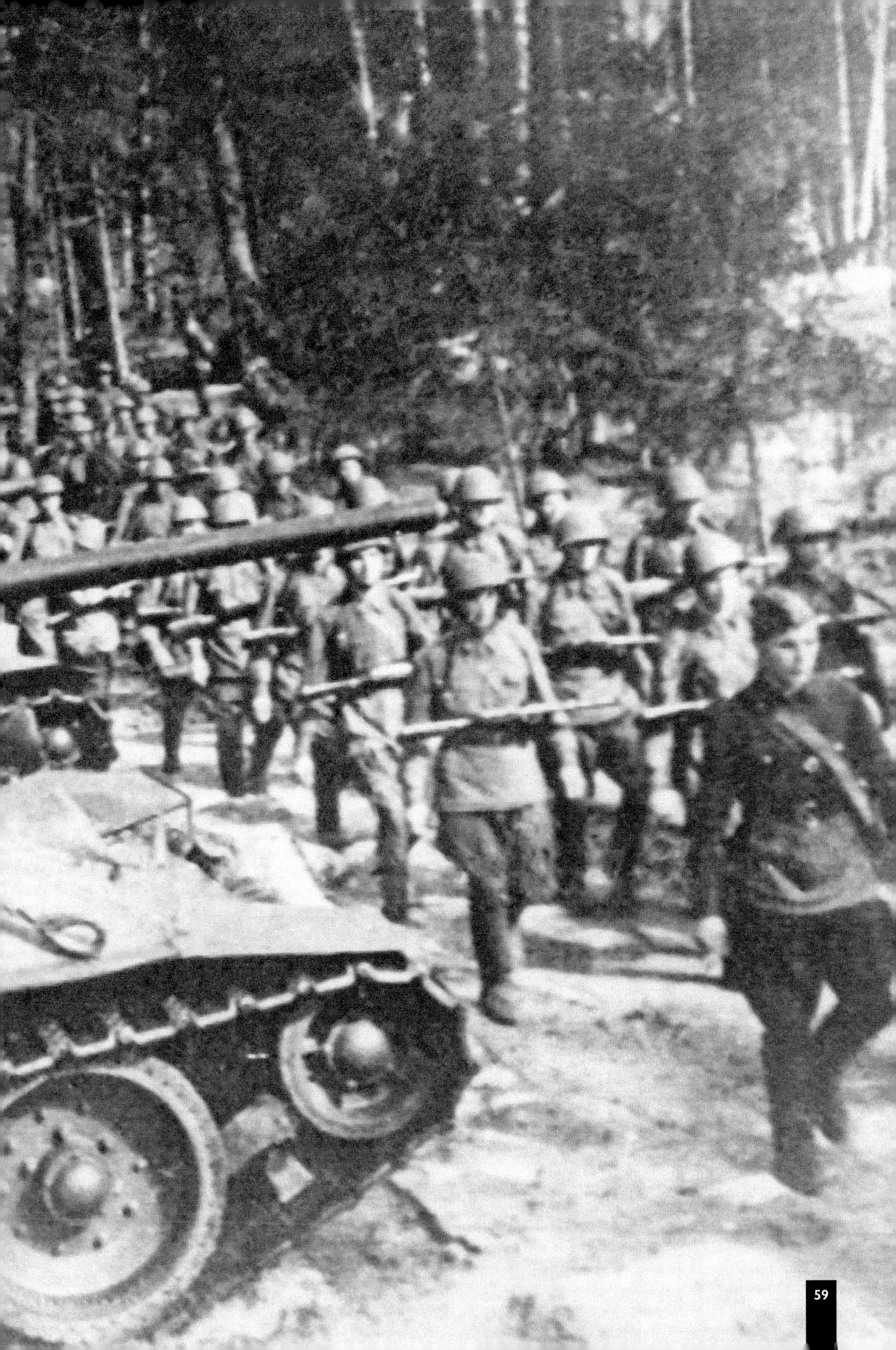

1944 US troops assault Omaha Beach during day one of the D-Day landings in Normandy, France, on June 6 1944. By the end of the day 34,000 troops had landed there. In total 160,000 were landed across all of the beaches by the Allies.

1944

This remarkable photograph from the air shows the American 4th division landing on Utah beach during the Normandy Landings on June 6 1944. D-Day was the largest seaborne invasion in history.

1944 *French refugees receive food from British troops in June 1944 during the Liberation of Normandy. More than two million Allied troops were in France by the end of August.*

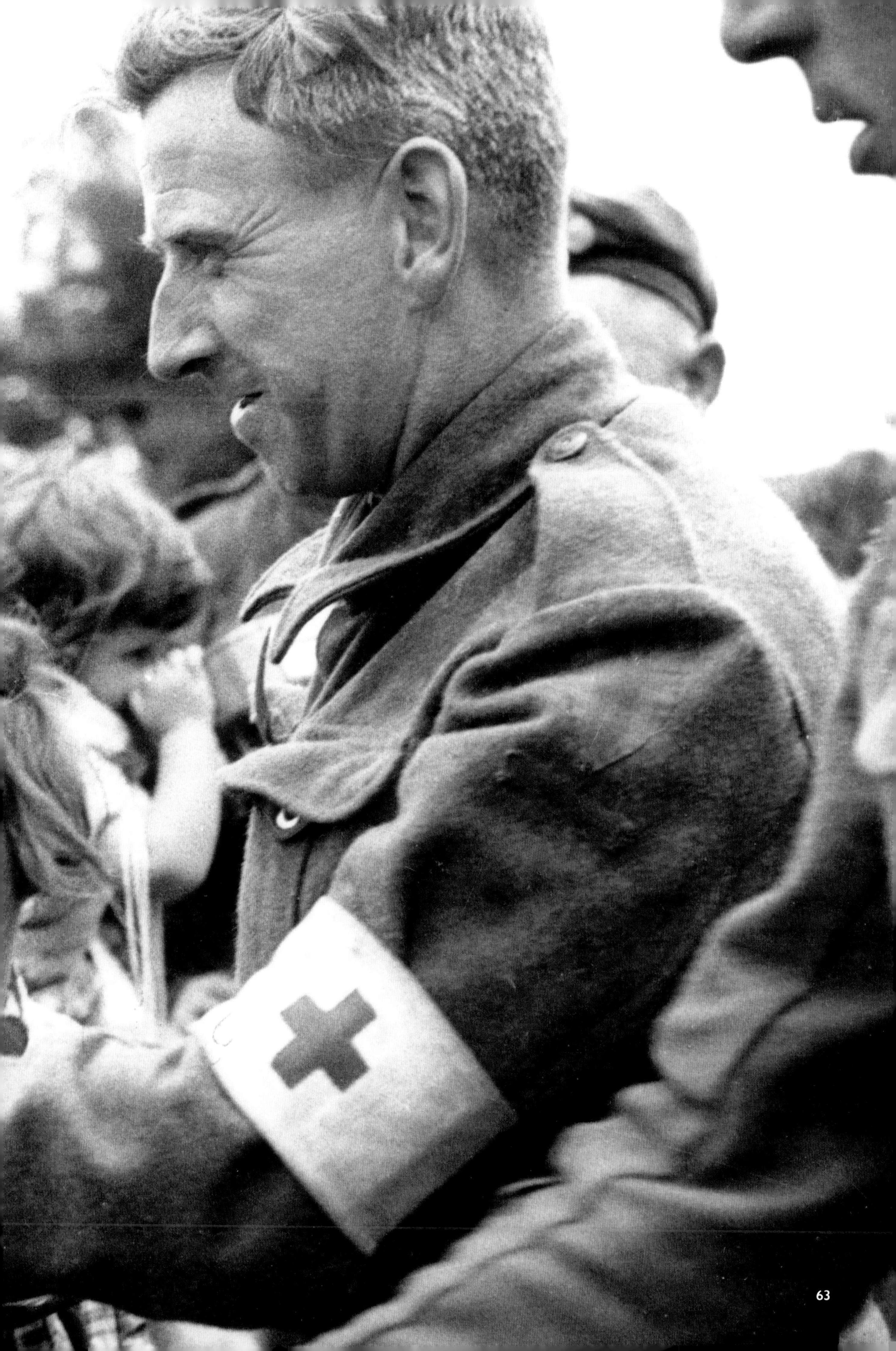

1944 *A soldier of the 101st Airborne Division of the First Allied Airborne Army unharnesses from his parachute and runs towards the assembly area for his unit in Holland during Operation Market Garden aimed at creating an invasion route into northern Germany in September 1944.*

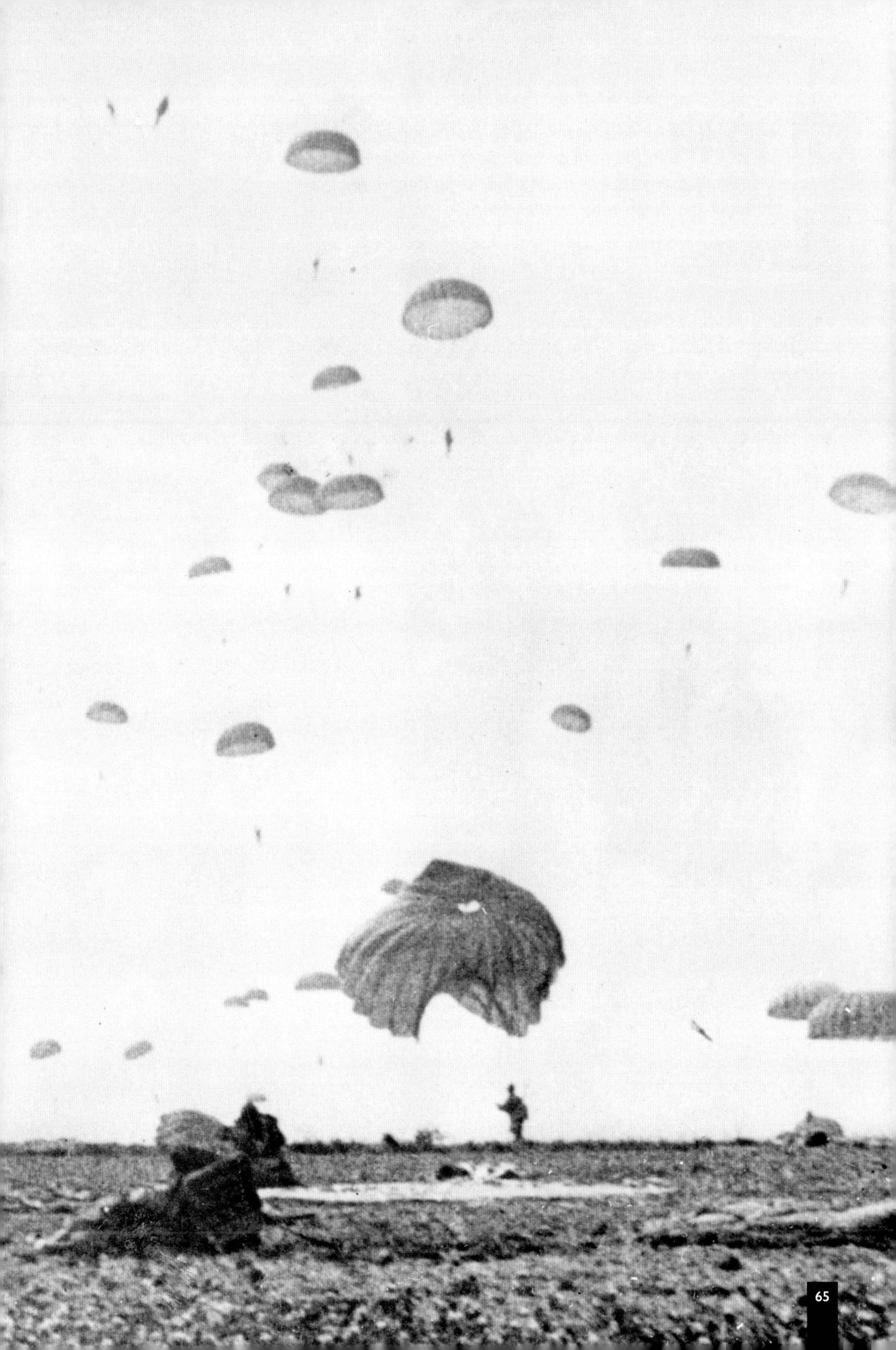

1944 American tanks and infantrymen on their way to the front pass through the village of Lierneux in Belgium. Lierneux was a site of fierce fighting during the Battle of the Bulge in December 1944.

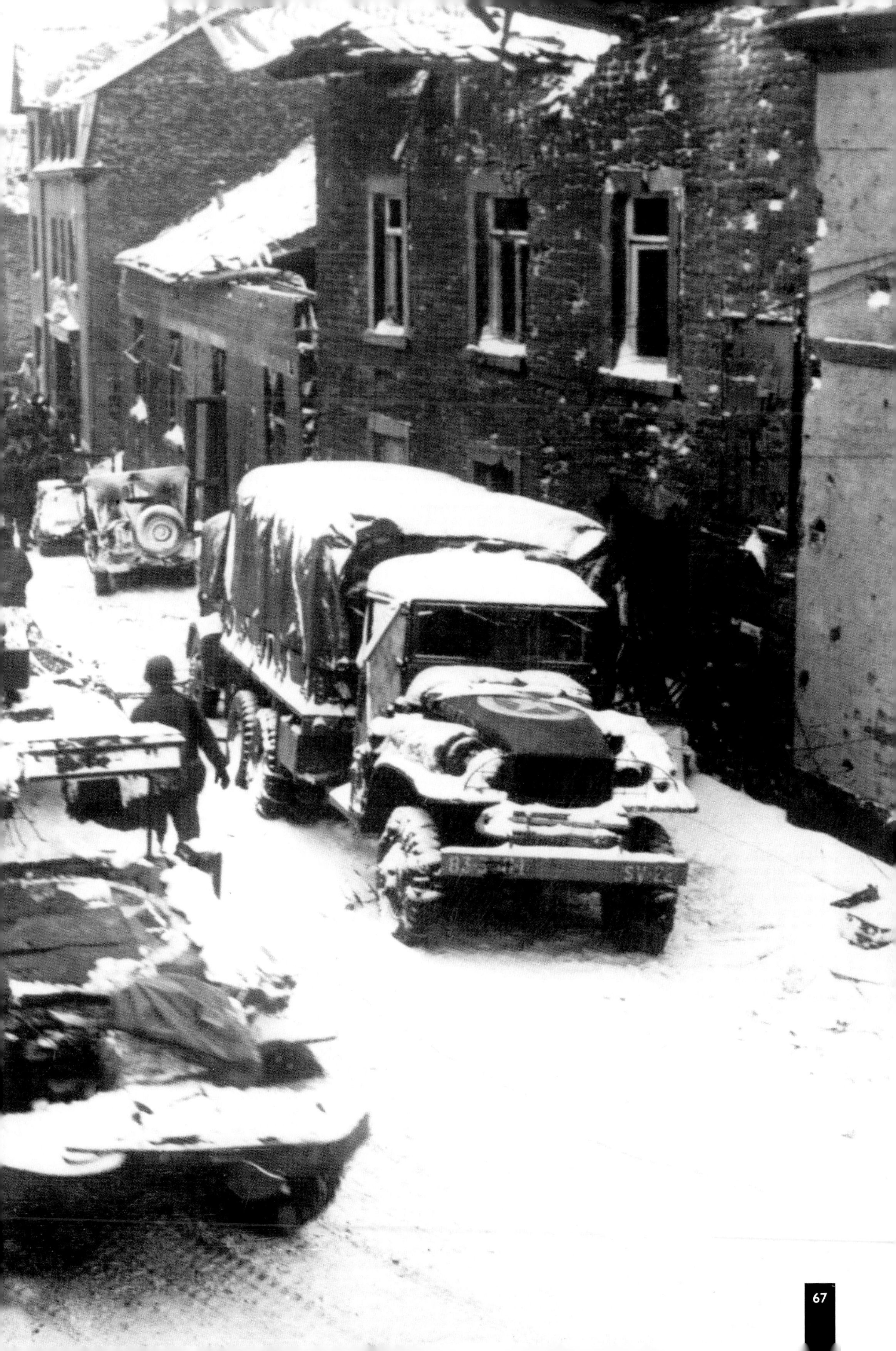

The Holocaust

General George Patton had witnessed the brutalities of war but what he saw at Ohrdruf concentration camp in southern Germany was enough to make him vomit.

Other deaths camps had been discovered by the Soviets but Ohrdruf was the first Nazi camp to be liberated by US forces. On April 12 1945, a week after the camp's liberation, Patton was one of three generals to visit. Few were then aware of the Holocaust so the trio were among the first to realise its true horrors. Corpses were scattered around, near charred human remains, and evidence of torture. Thirty emaciated bodies were discovered in a shed, covered with lime to cover the smell.

German citizens from the nearby town were forced to visit the camp and bury the dead. Within hours of this, the mayor of Ohrdruf and his wife hung themselves in their home.

This was just one camp and soon the world would learn of the systematic, mechanised mass murder of six million Jews by Nazi Germany. Millions of others were also targeted and killed, including Roma, disabled people, and gay people.

In a world where Holocaust denial is growing, International Holocaust Remembrance Day is ever more important. As survivor Elie Wiesel said: "To forget would not only be dangerous but offensive; to forget the dead would be akin to killing them a second time".

1945 *These Jewish children, with a nurse behind a barbed wire fence, are survivors of Auschwitz concentration camp, in Poland in February 1945 just days after the liberation of the camp by the Soviets. The children were dressed up with clothing from adult prisoners. Auschwitz was the largest Nazi extermination centre. More than 1.1 million men, women and children lost their lives here, many in gas chambers.*

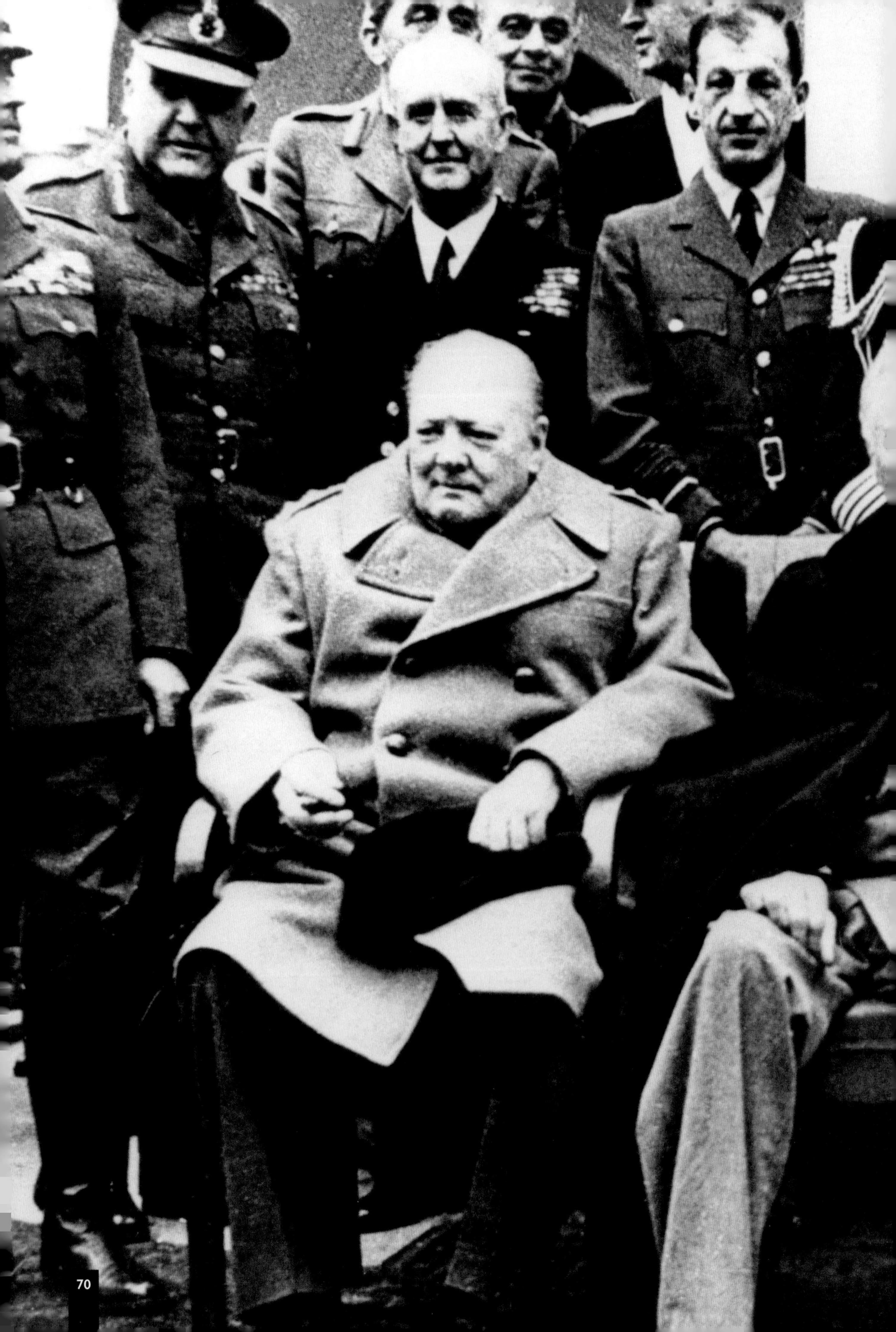

1945 *Three months before Germany's inevitable surrender in May 1945, the 'Big Three' world leaders - British Prime Minster Winston Churchill, US President Franklin Roosevelt and the USSR's Joseph Stalin - met at the Yalta Conference, in the Crimea, to decide the post-war world. They also sowed the seeds for the Iron Curtain and the Cold War.*

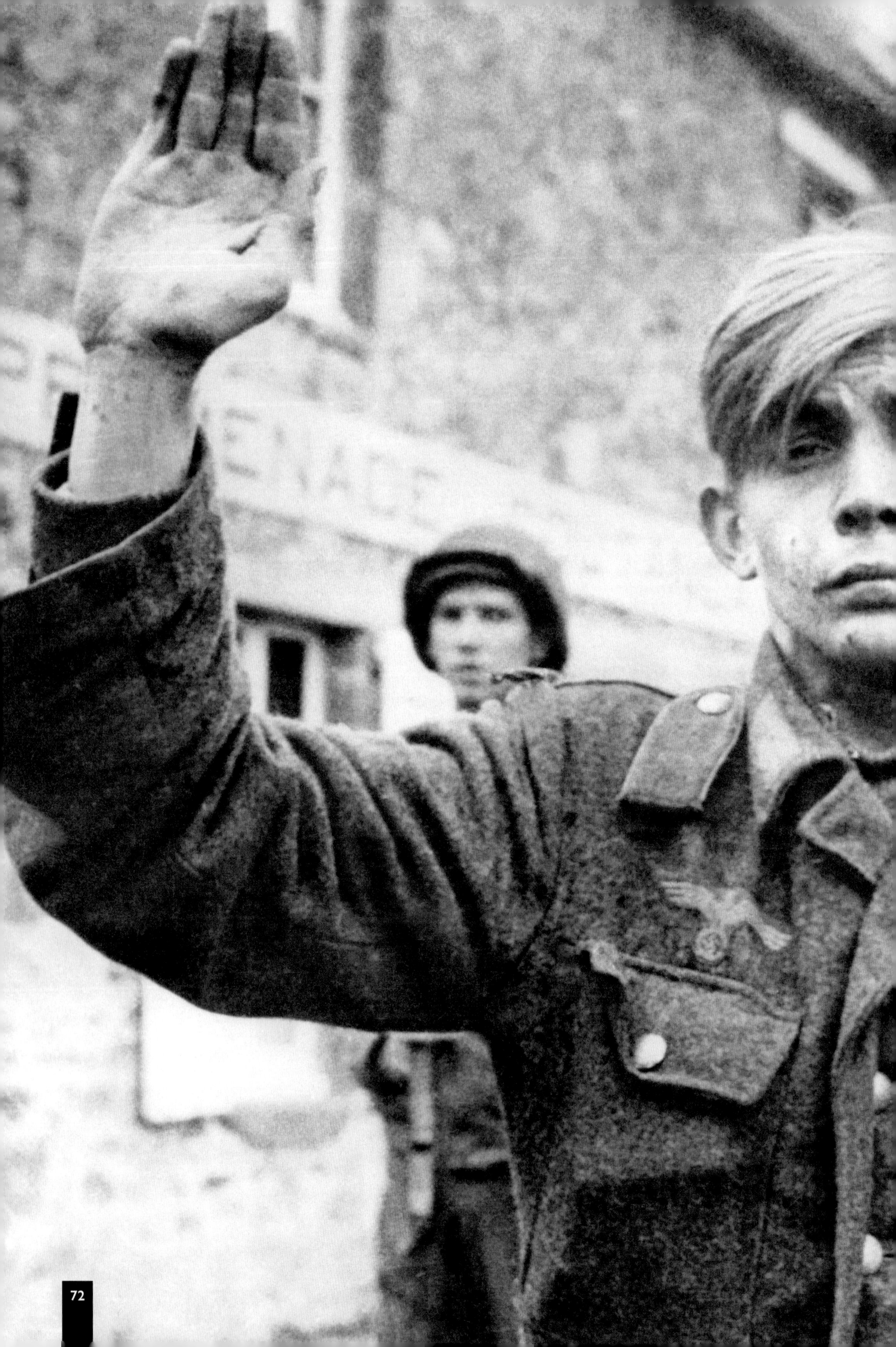

1944 *For him the war is over. This teenage German sniper surrenders on July 29 1944 after a fierce battle in and around the French town of Coutances as the American soldiers of VII and VIII Corps fought to break out of Normandy into the rest of France as part of Operation Cobra.*

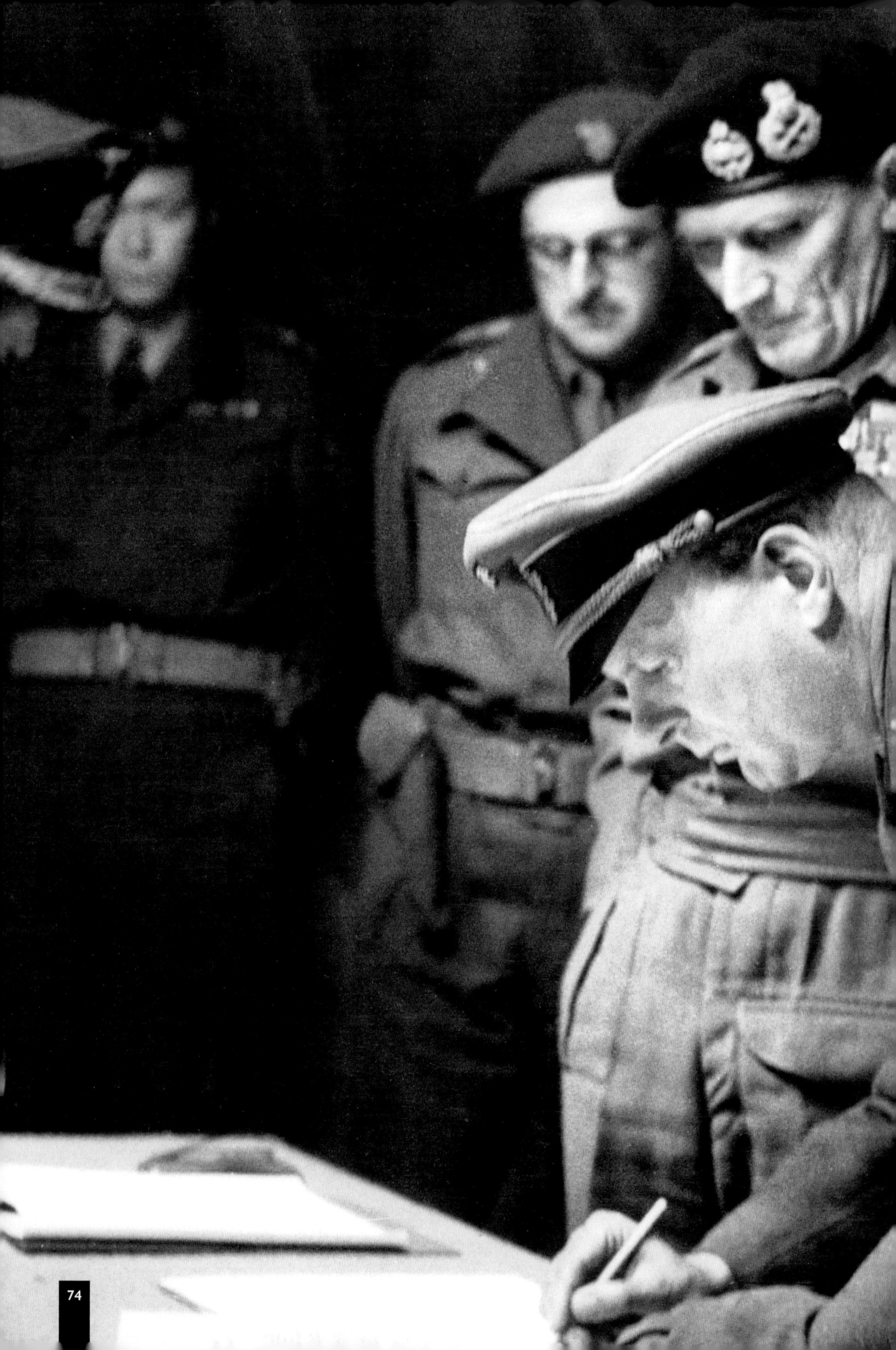

1945 German General Eberhard Kinzel puts his signature to the surrender of the German land, sea and air forces whilst British Field Marshal Bernard Montgomery watches on. Germany surrendered to the Allied forces on May 8 1945, ending the war in Europe.

1945 Soldiers of the Russian Red Army raising the hammer and sickle flag of the Soviet Union on the roof of Reichstag building in a devastated Berlin on May 2 1945 following the fall of the German capital.

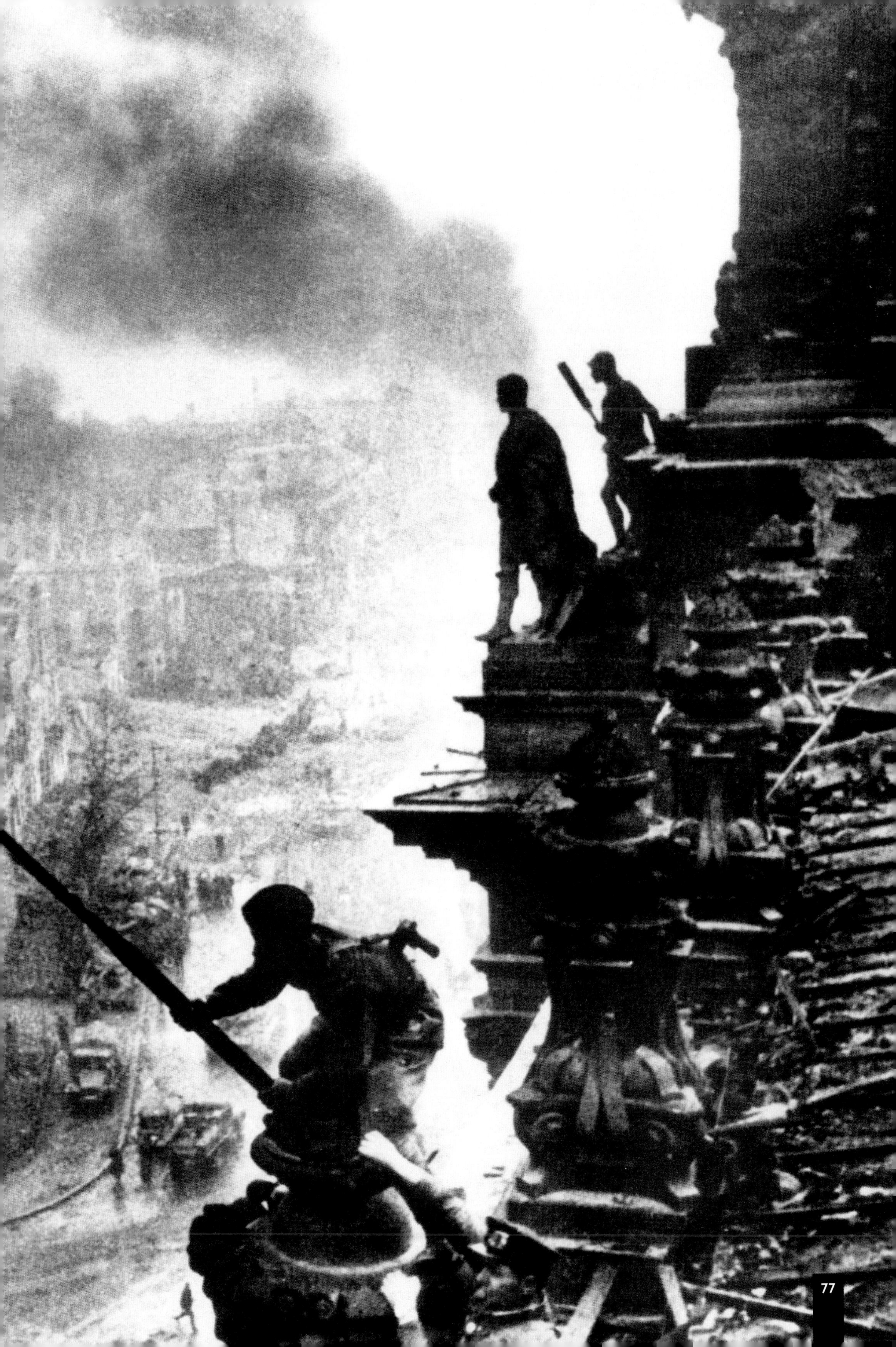

Victory

1945 *Prime Minister Winston Churchill joins Princess Elizabeth, Queen Elizabeth, King George VI and Princess Margaret on the balcony of Buckingham Palace during the VE Day celebrations in central London on May 8 1945.*

In south London they were placed in the shape of a 'V' for victory, as throughout the land tables were carried into the roads and avenues, piled with whatever food rationing would allow and street parties erupted.

The nation danced like never before not only to celebrate victory but peace after more than five years of war, and the imminent return home of those in the services lucky enough to have survived.

May 8 1945 had been declared a public holiday, and King George VI and Queen Elizabeth appeared on the balcony of Buckingham Palace many times with their daughters to cheering crowds. Princess Elizabeth and her sister Margaret were even allowed to sneak out and join the celebrations secretly in the crowd.

And Prime Minister Winston Churchill in a radio broadcast assured the ecstatic nation: "This is your victory!"

1945 After more than five and half years of war, rationing, death, and destruction, Britain let its hair down when Churchill declared May 8 1945 VE Day and a public holiday and partied like they never had before.

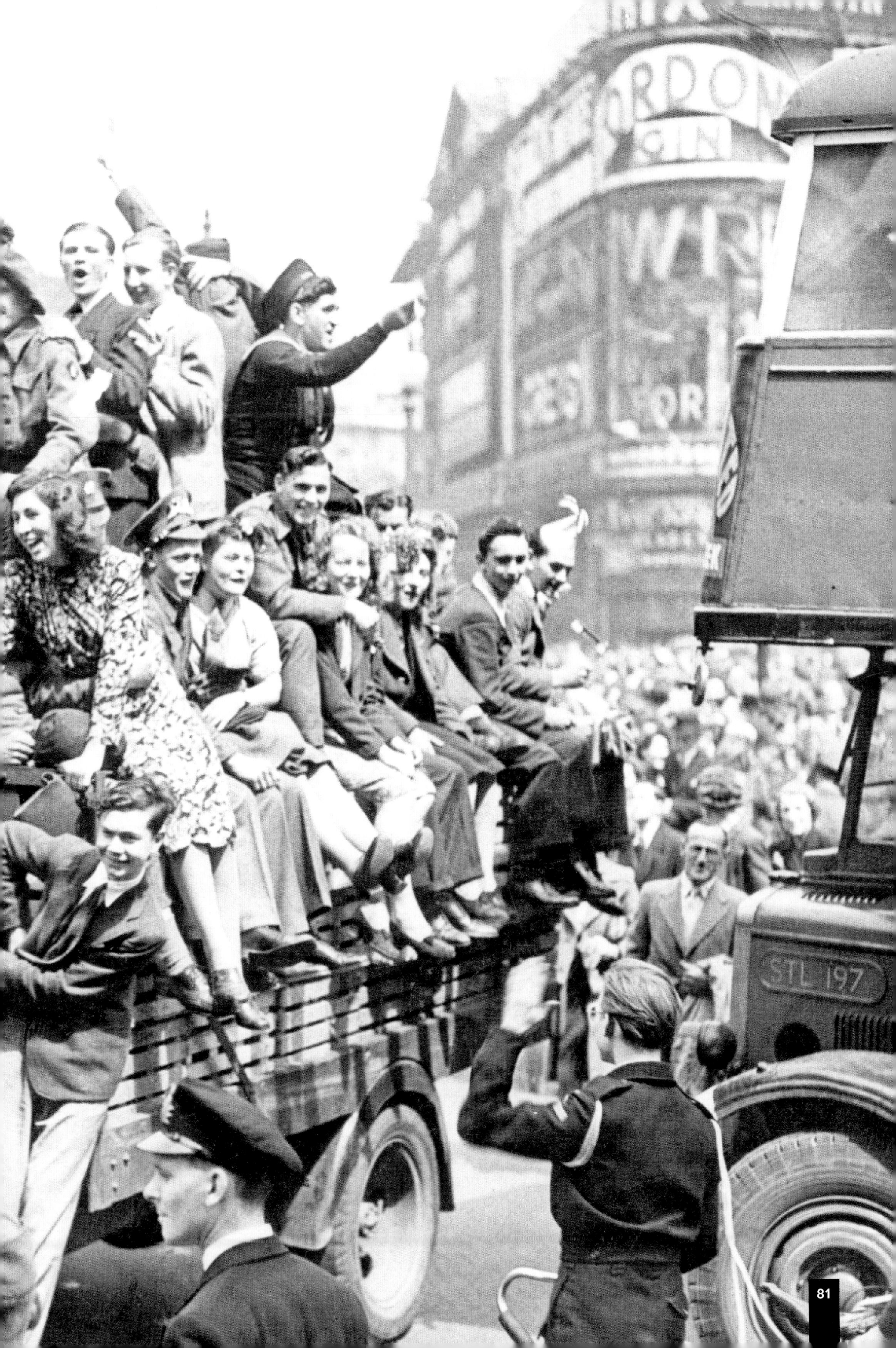
ORDON
GIN
STL 197

1945 A Kamikaze pilot of the Imperial Japanese Air Force in a suicide attack on the American navy warship USS Sangamon in the Pacific Ocean near Okinawa on May 4 1945.

1945 American landing craft land troops and supplies during the Battle of Okinawa on May 18 1945. The battle was the bloodiest and fiercest in the Pacific Ocean Theatre, with some 50,000 Allied and around 100,000 Japanese casualties.

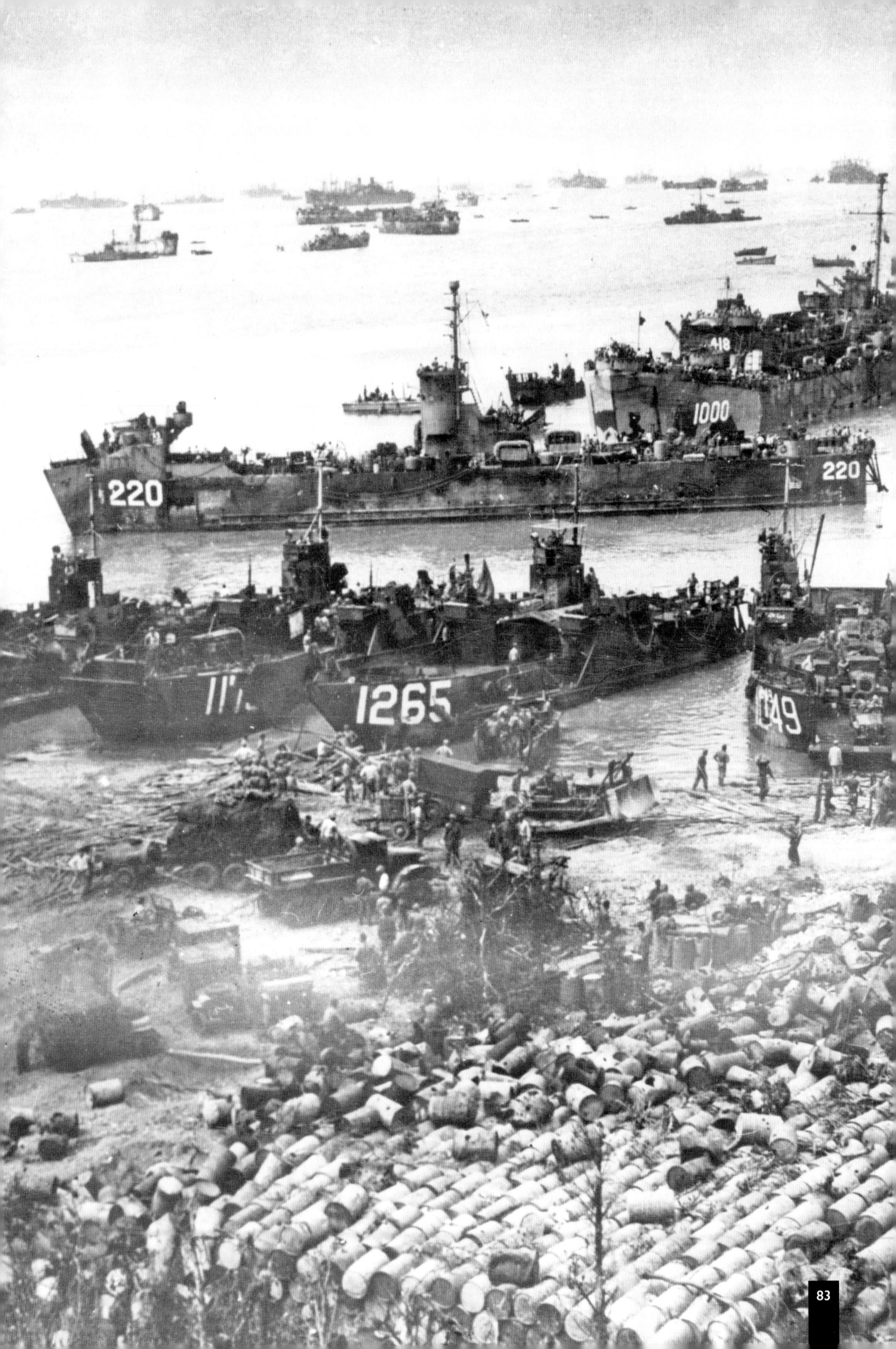
220
1000
418
220
1265

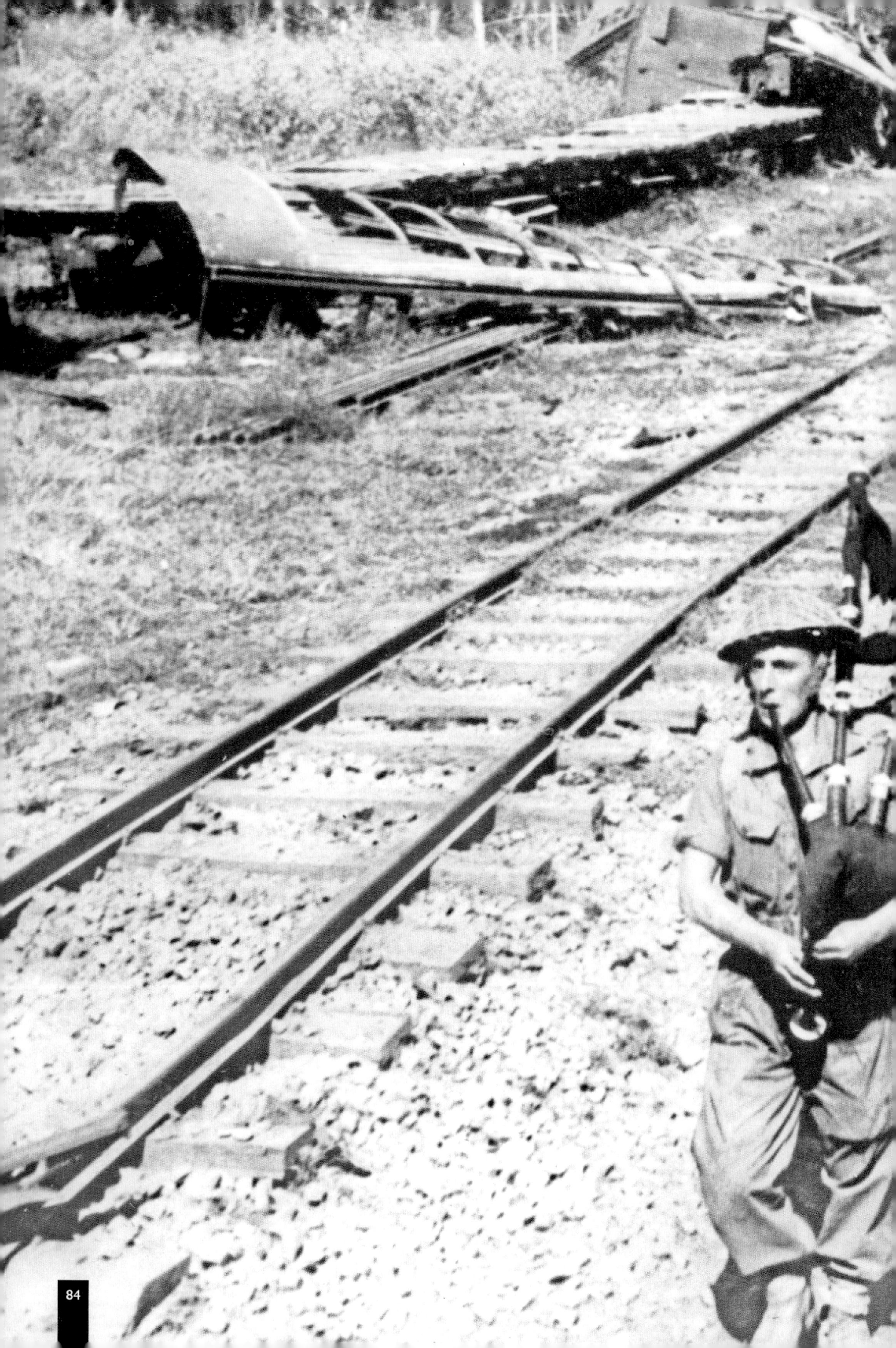

1944 Piper John McLean leads the men of "D" Company, 1st Battalion Royal Scots Fusiliers to the tune of "Cock o' the North" as they march alongside a railway to celebrate both St Andrew's Day and the ending of the Japanese occupation of Pinwe in North Burma on November 30 1944.

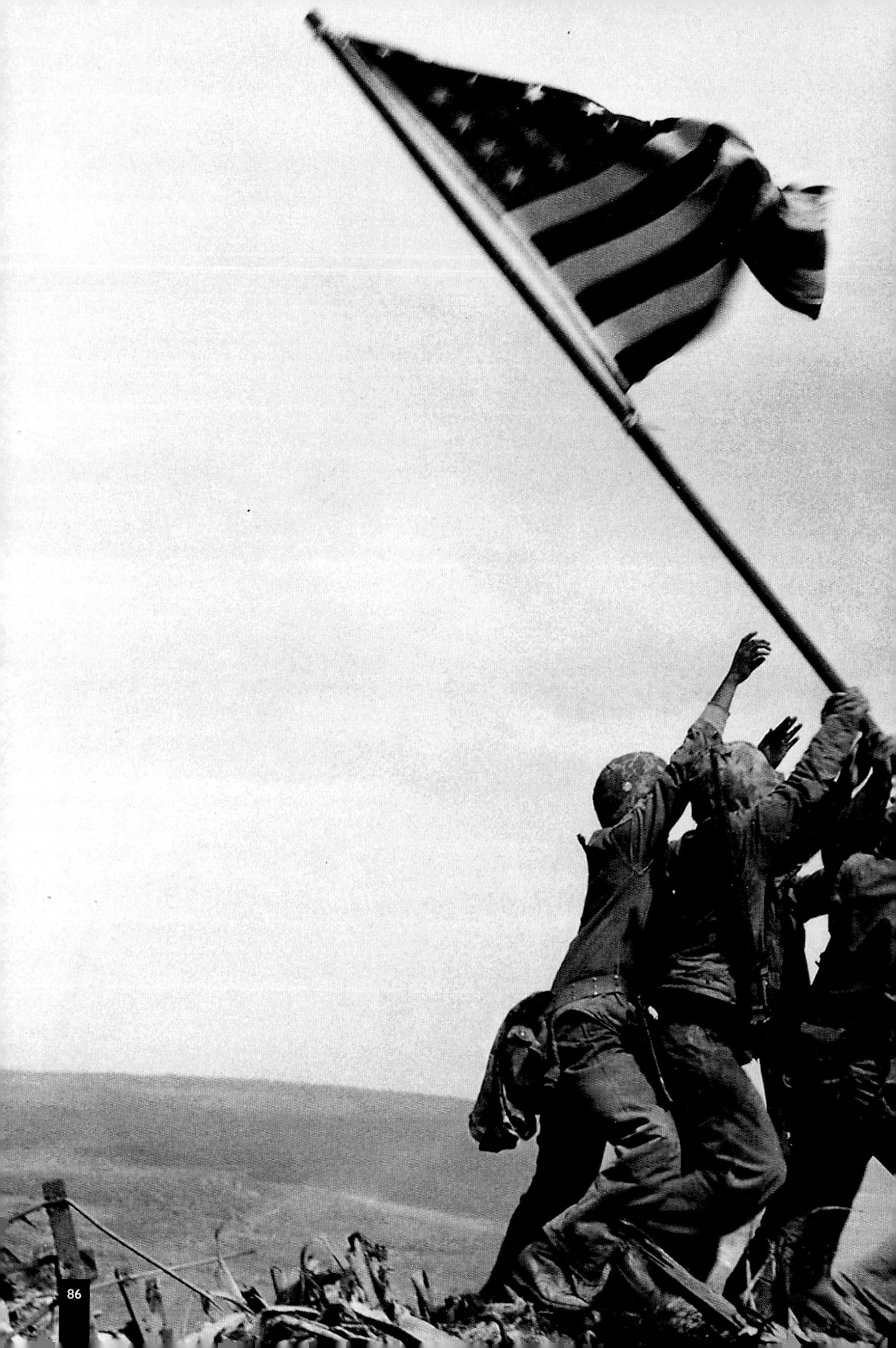

1945 *Photographer Joe Rosenthal captured this iconic photograph "Raising the Flag on Iwo Jima". It shows six US Marines raising the Stars and Stripes on Mount Suribachi, the island's highest peak on February 23 1945. The victory came at a cost – during a five-week battle there were three American casualties for every two Japanese.*

Nagasaki and Hiroshima

Yasujiro Tanaka was just over two miles from ground zero of the Nagasaki atomic bomb.

Aged just three when it was dropped by the USAF onto the Japanese city on August 9 1945, he later remembered "my surroundings turned blindingly white, like a million camera flashes going off at once. Then, pitch darkness. I was buried alive under the house. When my uncle finally found me I was unconscious. My face was misshapen. He was certain that I was dead.

"Thankfully, I survived. But since that day, mysterious scabs began to form all over my body. More than a decade after the bombing, my mother began to notice glass shards growing out of her skin – debris from the day of the bombing. 'What did I do to the Americans?' she would often say, 'Why did they do this to me?'"

The simple answer is to end the fighting. By mid-1945, the war in Europe was over, but Japan was still fighting fiercely. Although losing, Japan showed no signs of surrendering. The US feared a full-scale invasion of mainland Japan could result in hundreds of thousands of US casualties.

Some Americans also wanted revenge for Pearl Harbor and the terrible treatment of prisoners of war.

With Japan not offering unconditional surrender, the US believed only a shockingly powerful act could force a change. In the end it took two - an atomic bomb on Hiroshima on August 6, followed by Nagasaki three days later.

At noon on August 15, Japanese Emperor Hirohito broadcast a surrender message to his people on the radio.

1945 On August 9 1945 the United States dropped an atomic bomb nicknamed 'Fat Man' on the Japanese city of Nagasaki, killing more than 150,000 people. Coming three days after the atomic bombing of Hiroshima, it led to the Japanese surrender on August 15.

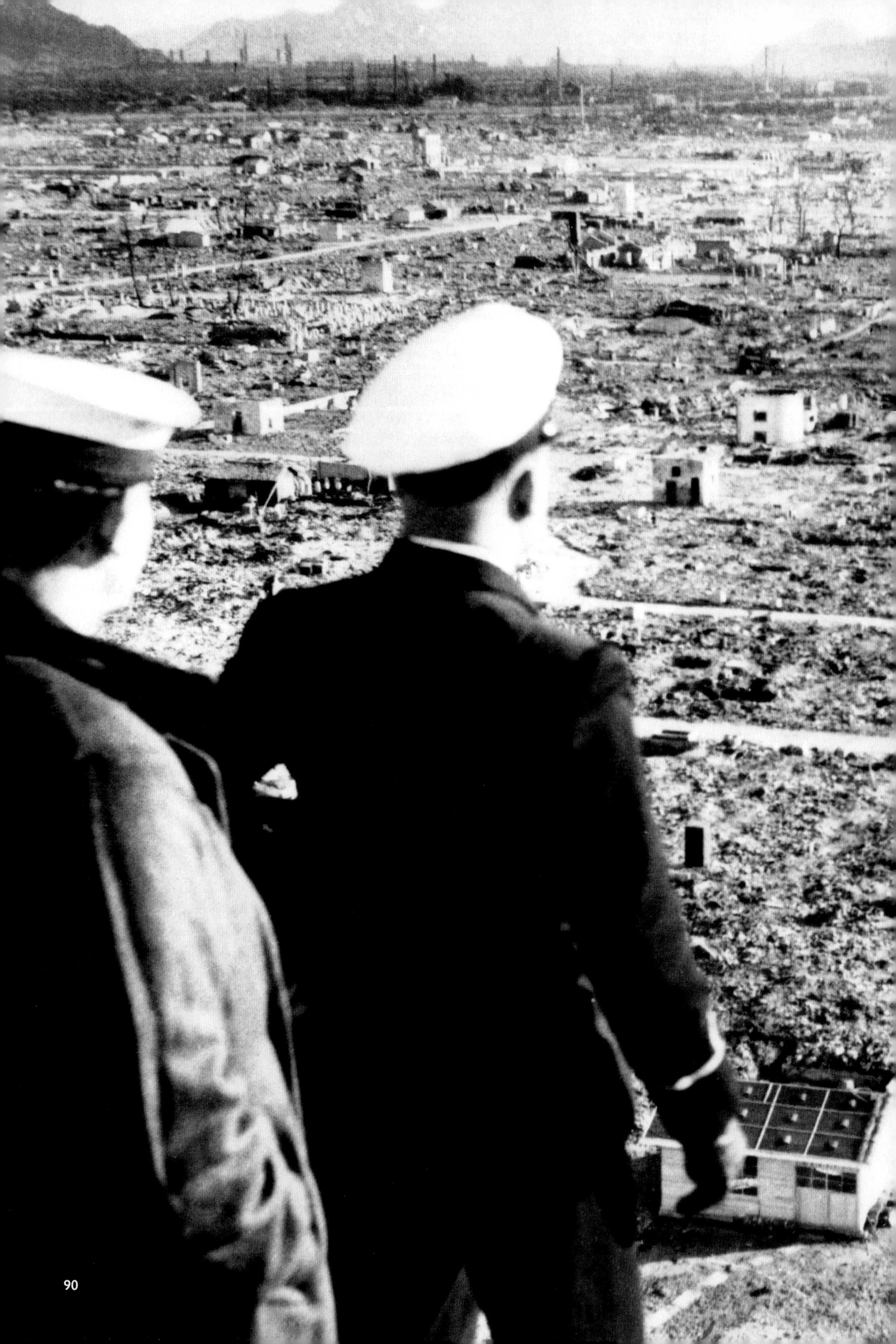

1945 A Royal Navy officer and rating look across the destruction of Hiroshima several weeks after the dropping of the 'Little Boy' atomic bomb on Monday August 6 1945. The explosion killed an estimated 80,000 people. By the end of the year, injury and radiation had killed an estimated further 70,000.

1945 *Japanese prisoners of war are washed by Lance Corporal Smith after they were taken captive by British forces during fighting along the Toungoo-Pegu road in Burma (now Myanmar) as they attempted to reach Siam (now Thailand) in August 1945.*

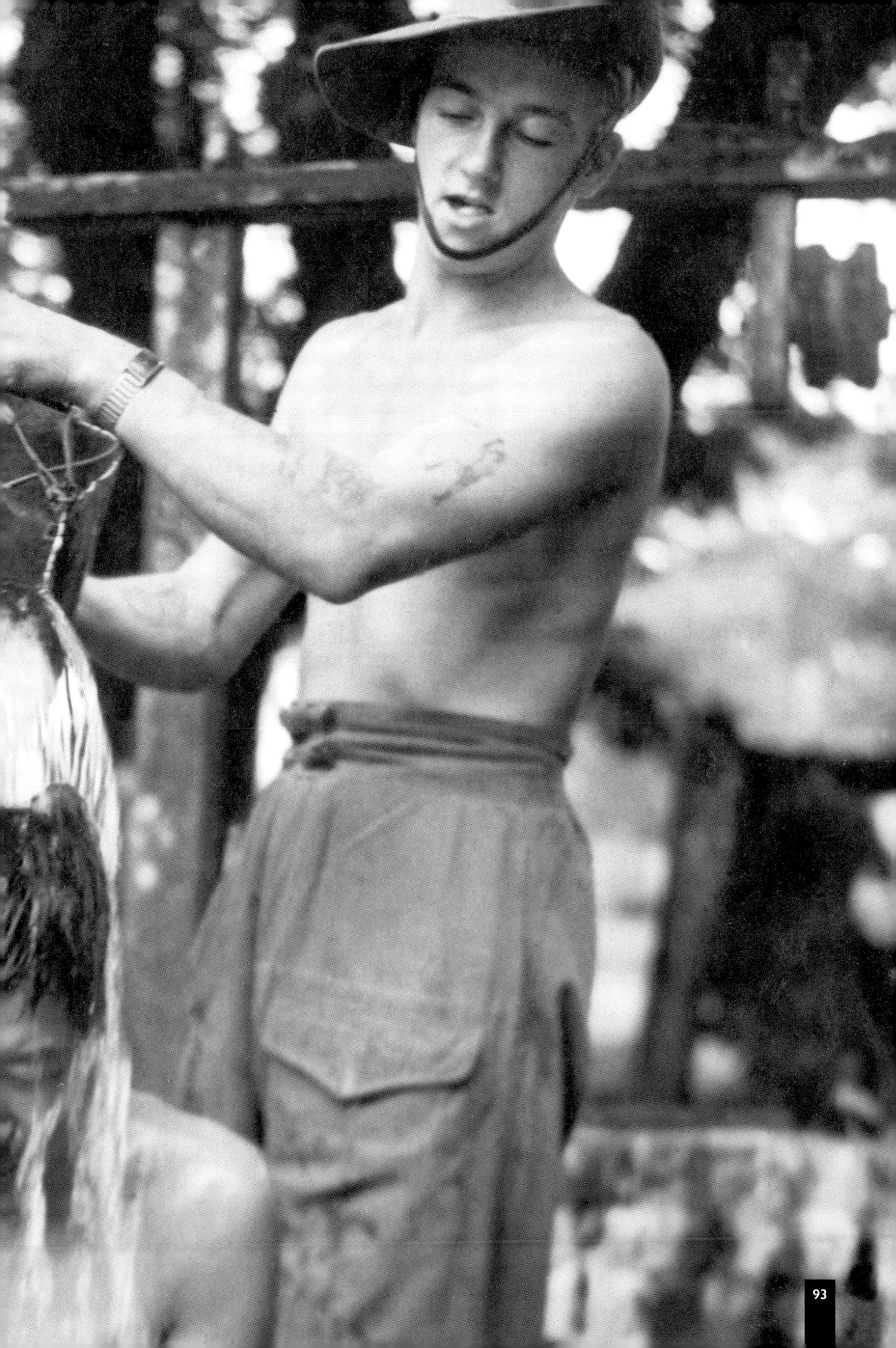

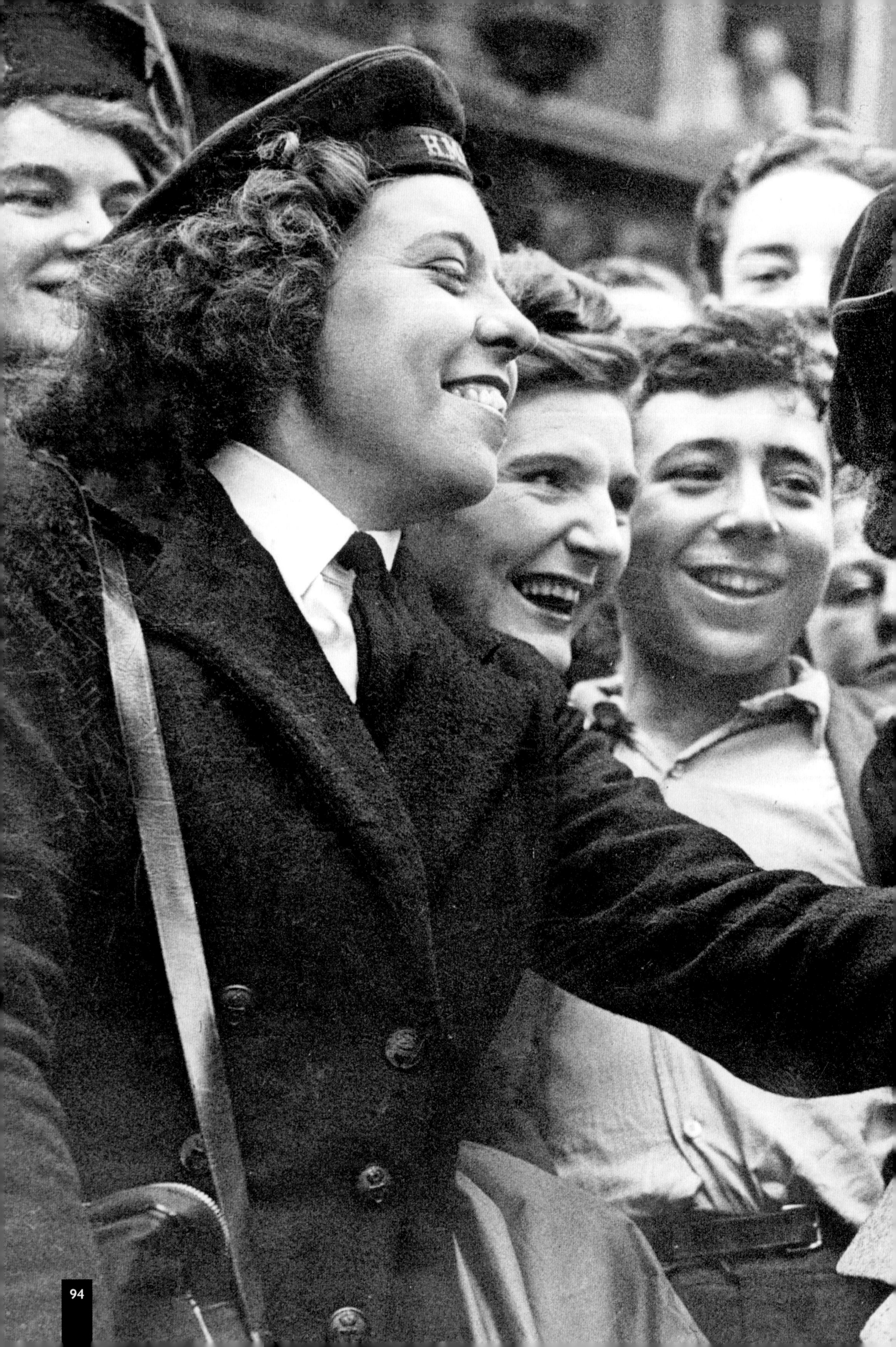
HM

1945 *She'd been worried about her army lieutenant husband fighting somewhere in China, but Mrs Lotus Lee-Chang (Lulu to her friends) is congratulated by WRENS about news of Japan's collapse during Victory over Japan Day celebrations in Liverpool on August 15 1945.*

1945 It wasn't just British troops fighting for King and Country. More than three million troops from what we now know as the Commonwealth put their lives at risk to fight the Nazi threat, often with incredible bravery. Pictured here are three recipients of the Victoria Cross after an investiture at Buckingham Palace, on October 16 1945. Left to right: Naik Bhabbhagta Gurung of the 2nd Gurkha Rifles, Naik Gian Singh of the 15th Punjab Regiment and Havildar Umrao Singh of the Indian Artillery.